The True Cost of Food

Contents

Food and Us 2
Global Warming 4
Food Miles 6
Animal Farming 10
Commercial Fishing 14
Water Consumption 18
Chemical Sprays 20
Fertilisers 20
Pesticides 22
Making a Difference 24
Slow Food 26

Food and Us

Behind every environmental problem, food is a contributing factor.

Our demand for food to feed our huge world population **has caused air and water pollution,** deforestation, erosion and lack of fresh water. It has also threatened some animal species and contributed to climate change.

Before the start of industrial food production, people ate locally produced fresh foods. Meat was expensive and eaten in moderation.

CLARIFY

deforestation
moderation
environmentally-conscious

PREDICT

"Behind every environmental problem, food is a contributing factor."
How do you think the author will support/validate this statement?

BUT ALL THIS COMES AT A COST TO THE ENVIRONMENT

Over the last century, diets in the Western world have changed dramatically. Food can be produced more cheaply and quickly using modern animal and crop farming methods. Cheaper and easier transport methods have allowed food to be exported around the world and often sold more cheaply than local produce. Fast food giants sell millions of hamburgers every day, dramatically increasing the demand for cheap beef and putting pressure on the farming industry.

All this comes at a cost to the environment. Unless we start to change our food-buying habits and make environmentally-conscious food decisions,

our planet faces a grim future.

AUTHOR PURPOSE

Why do you think the author might have written this book?

Global Warming

CLARIFY
greenhouse gases
methane
nitrous oxide
large-scale change

One of the **biggest threats** to the future of the planet is **global warming**.

Scientific studies indicate recent years have been the hottest on record and scientists predict that the Earth will continue to heat up in the years to come. As a result, sea levels are rising and the world is seeing an increase in **EXTREME WEATHER EVENTS**, such as droughts, floods, heat waves and hurricanes.

PREDICT
How will changes to the way we produce food affect global warming?

Global warming is also endangering penguins, seals, walruses, fish, elephants, frogs, butterflies, birds and many other animals, including humans. Increasing temperatures could also lead to a rising number of mosquitoes and serious tropical diseases worldwide.

Most scientists agree that global warming is caused by human activity that releases **GREENHOUSE GASES** into the atmosphere. These gases include carbon dioxide, methane and nitrous oxide. One of the biggest contributors to global warming is the production of food. A large-scale change in our approach to how we produce food would be an important step towards bringing global warming under control.

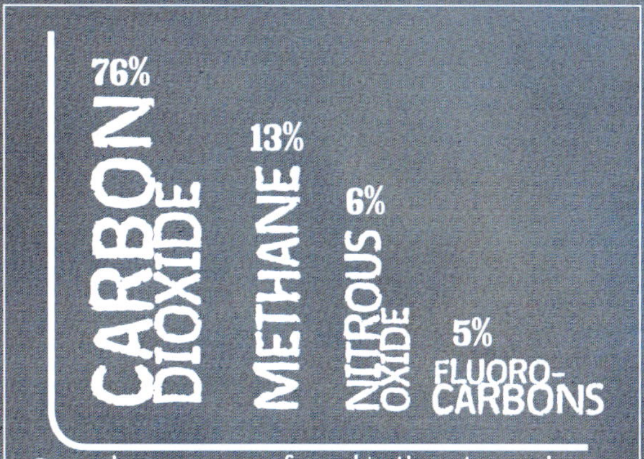

Greenhouse gases found in the atmosphere

ONE OF THE BIGGEST CONTRIBUTORS TO GLOBAL WARMING IS THE PRODUCTION

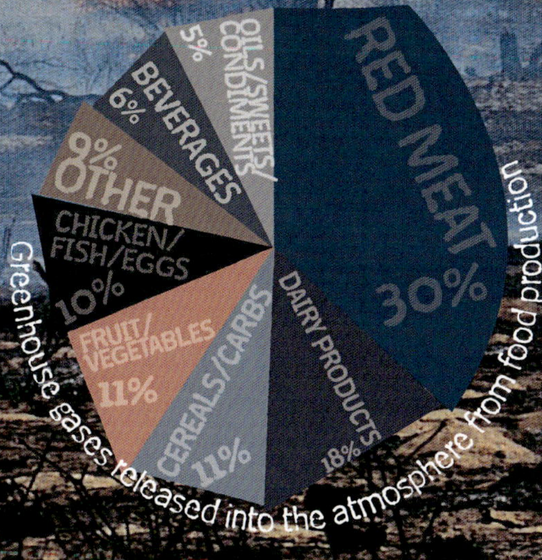

Greenhouse gases released into the atmosphere from food production

BIAS

Is bias evident in the author's perspective? Why/why not?

Food Miles

"Food miles" is a term that refers to the distance food travels from its producer to the consumer who buys it.

CLARIFY
globalisation
carbon gases

Today, in an age of globalisation, food is shipped **thousands of kilometres** around the world **every day**.

People living in countries with cooler climates can eat fruit and vegetables grown in sunnier countries. Local supermarkets and speciality stores stock food from Asia, Europe, Africa and South America to meet the demands of Westerners' changing food tastes.

Although many people enjoy the variety of food now available to them, it does come at a cost to the environment. Food has to be transported by truck, train, ship, aeroplane or a combination of these. All these methods of transport use vast amounts of fossil fuels.

Take the example of a family living in Canada or New Zealand buying fresh strawberries from California. These berries will be transported from the farm to a warehouse in a large **truck**, then from the warehouse to the airport in **another truck**. There they will be loaded onto an **aeroplane** and flown to a major airport. From the airport they are put on a **truck** and delivered to a main warehouse before being loaded onto a **train** and delivered to another warehouse.

VISUAL FEATURES

The transportation of strawberries
How would you interpret the textual information visually?

Then they are put onto a **truck** and delivered to the supermarket, where the family picks them up and drives them home in their **car**. Each of these steps produces carbon gases that contribute to global warming.

ISSUES

Should people boycott food produced in other countries? What could be the effect on the economies of poorer countries if wealthier countries boycotted their food?

Cost is another factor in food export. It is often cheaper to import food from countries where labour is cheap than to produce it locally.

BEYOND THE TEXT

What are the repercussions of the globalisation of food for people in developing countries?

CLARIFY

carbon footprint
nutritional value

By choosing to eat locally grown and produced foods, we can **reduce our carbon footprint.**

Local farmers' markets are a good place to buy fresh, locally grown fruit and vegetables.

It's also important to read labels on meat, dairy and other food products to be aware of how far they have travelled.

The distance the consumer travels to buy food also counts as food miles. A "locavore" is a term for someone who will only buy food that has been produced and sold **within a 160-kilometre radius of where they live.**

POINT OF VIEW

Suggest an alternative point of view on the information presented?

PRODUCE SHIPPED FROM OVERSEAS COULD BE MONTHS OLD

REDUCE OUR CARBON FOOTPRINT

Eating locally grown food is also often better for you. When fruit or vegetables are harvested they start losing their nutritional value and should be eaten as soon as possible. If you buy produce from a farmers' market or good local shop it will probably be no more than a few days old, whereas produce shipped from overseas could be months old.

RESEARCH

When food products contain imported goods from unspecified countries, how can you ascertain the country of origin?

Animal Farming

CLARIFY

flatulence
ammonia
hydrogen sulphide
algae blooms
cryptosporidium

One of the biggest contributors to global warming is **animal-based farming.**

Animal farming causes approximately 18 percent of the greenhouse gas emissions that lead to global warming. By comparison, all forms of transportation on the planet combined produce about 13.5 percent of emissions.

ANIMAL FARMING ALSO POLLUTES WATERWAYS AND CONTRIBUTES TO DEFORESTATION.

Through belching and flatulence, cattle produce large amounts of the greenhouse gases methane, carbon dioxide and nitrous oxide. They also produce ammonia, which contributes to acid rain, and hydrogen sulphide, which has been blamed for past mass extinctions on Earth and can cause brain damage or death in humans in high doses.

The greenhouse gas emissions arising every year from the production and consumption of cheeseburgers in the United States alone is roughly the amount emitted by 6.5 million to 19.6 million sports utility vehicles.

The demand for meat and dairy products in the Western world is high, especially in the United States, where the average person consumes 124 kilograms of meat, including 44 kilograms of beef, a year. To keep up with this demand, farmers have developed more and more efficient farming methods.

But these methods come at a cost to the environment.

RESEARCH

"Animal farming causes approximately 18 percent of the greenhouse gas emissions that lead to global warming."
What evidence can you find to support this statement?

CATTLE produce GREENHOUSE GASES

In many countries, cattle are raised on factory farms. They are kept indoors in huge warehouses, where they are fattened up for slaughter. Hundreds of thousands of pigs, chickens or cows are crammed into these buildings and produce huge amounts of waste, sometimes as much as that of a small city.

This waste not only releases large amounts of greenhouse gases and other pollutants into the air, it also pollutes waterways, contaminating drinking water and killing millions of fish. Ammonia gas from animal waste can be carried more than 480 kilometres through the air before landing in waterways, where it causes algae blooms and kills fish. Algae blooms use up oxygen in the water and create "dead zones" where there is not enough oxygen for ocean life. In the Gulf of Mexico, there is a dead zone thousands of square kilometres in size.

EMOTIVE APPEAL

How has the author used emotive language to persuade you to a particular viewpoint?

Animal waste is also dangerous to humans, causing many different diseases and health problems, from short-term memory loss to miscarriages in pregnant women and even death. Manure from dairy cows is thought to have contributed to an outbreak of cryptosporidium in an American town's drinking water one year, killing more than 100 people and making 400,000 sick.

AUTHOR PURPOSE

Do you think the author has used information to manipulate or influence your ideas about animal farming? Why/why not?

Cows are naturally grass-eaters

and have a complex system of stomachs designed for eating grass. However, factory-farmed cattle are fed a combination of corn, liquefied fat, protein supplements, alfalfa hay and silage.

This diet causes many different health problems, such as bloat, which happens when a stomach part called the rumen inflates like a balloon until it presses against the cow's lungs, suffocating it. Another common problem resulting from this diet is an infected liver,

which can also lead to death.

Factory farmers try to reduce these health problems by feeding their animals large amounts of antibiotics. In the United States, 70 percent of the antibiotics manufactured are fed to cows.

This overuse of antibiotics adds to the possibility that super bugs will form that have an immunity to antibiotics. A super bug could cause widespread illness and death among humans.

RESEARCH

"In the United States, 70 percent of the antibiotics manufactured are fed to cows." Do you accept this statement? Why/why not? What evidence can you find to support this statement.

QUESTION GENERATE

What questions do you have about this information?

Deforestation and land degradation are other environmental concerns caused by cattle farming.

Thirty percent of the Earth's land surface is used for grazing animals

and to grow crops for their feed. In Latin America, 70 percent of what was once rainforest is now being used for cattle grazing.

Once land has been used for cattle farming over a period of time, it can become degraded. Because of overgrazing, erosion and compacting of the earth by hooves, the land loses its nutrients and dries up. In some places, the land turns to desert. About 20 percent of the world's pastureland is now degraded. Once degradation has happened, the land can no longer be used for growing crops or replanting felled forests.

AUTHOR PURPOSE

Is the author's presentation of information balanced/ unbalanced? Why?

ONCE DEGRADATION HAS HAPPENED, THE LAND CAN NO LONGER BE USED

Commerical Fishing

> **CLARIFY**
> cyanide poisoning
> ecosystems

Commercial fishing is another human activity that is causing serious harm to the environment. Fish and other seafood are being overfished at an alarming rate. More than 75 percent of the world's fisheries are now either fully fished or overfished.

There are many different methods of commercial fishing, many of which are very wasteful. They catch huge amounts of fish at a time, including unwanted fish, called by-catch. Worldwide, 25 percent of fish caught commercially is thrown away.

One of the worst examples is shrimp harvesting in the Gulf of Mexico, **where around 80 percent of what is caught is unwanted.**

Longline fishing is a very destructive fishing method used to catch large fish such as tuna and swordfish. This method uses a main fishing line with attached branch lines, each fitted with one or more hooks. Many other types of unwanted animals are caught on the lines. Over the last 18 years, around 89 percent of hammerhead sharks and 80 percent of thresher and white sharks have disappeared from the north-east Atlantic Ocean, and that is thought to be mostly due to longline fishing. As many as 250,000 endangered loggerhead turtles and critically endangered leatherback turtles are caught on longlines every year.

> **ISSUE**
> **Should destructive fishing practices be banned?**
> Why/why not? What social action could you take to protest against these wasteful practices?

Longline fishing also kills more than **300,000 seabirds** each year. The birds are attracted to the bait on the lines and get caught by hooks and drowned. Around 26 species of seabirds, including 17 albatross species, are threatened with extinction because of longline fishing.

INFERENCE

What can you infer about the commercial operators who use harmful methods of fishing?

Another destructive fishing method is bottom trawling. This is where large weighted nets are dragged along the ocean floor, picking up and destroying everything in their way. This method results in the deaths of huge numbers of unwanted fish and kills other ocean animals, such as dolphins, turtles, penguins, seals and whales.

Some fishing practices are **so damaging** they are illegal. However, this doesn't stop people from using them. In some countries, dynamite is used on coral reefs to kill fish. These explosions cause a lot of damage to coral reefs and can kill fish within a radius of 50 metres or more from the blast. Reefs in parts of South-east Asia have been completely destroyed by dynamite fishing.

Another illegal fishing method used in South-east Asia is cyanide poisoning. Cyanide poison is used to stun fish, which are then taken to aquariums or sold live at fish markets. Cyanide kills coral and young fish, causing long-term damage to delicate coral ecosystems.

75 PERCENT OF THE WORLD'S FISHERIES ARE NOW EITHER FULLY FISHED OR OVERFISHED

VISUAL FEATURES

How could you interpret the information on destructive fishing methods in a visual summary?

FISH CAUGHT WITH A HAND-LINE OR HARPOONED, AND HAND-GATHERED SHELLFISH, ARE ALSO MUCH LESS HARMFUL

CLARIFY
sustainable seafood

Overfishing is also affecting the ocean's ecosystem. Over the last 30 years, as the world's population has grown, the demand for seafood has doubled. Populations of large predatory fish such as marlin, tuna and swordfish are now a 10th of what they were 50 years ago. By-catch often includes small fish that, if they had been given the chance to grow older and breed, could have helped to replenish fish populations.

As the populations of large predatory fish have declined, humans have gained an appetite for smaller fish. Thirty years ago, fish that were once used for bait, such as hagfish and squid, have become popular eating fish. Scientists see this as a worrying trend, as we are eating our way down the ocean's food web.

READER RESPONSE
What feelings were evoked by the information in this chapter?

The ocean's ecosystem is a complex system. For every species that becomes extinct, there may be several others that rely on it for food. Birds such as the African penguin are having difficulty finding enough fish to feed their young as fish supplies are depleted.

QUESTION

Can the world's rising demand for seafood be met by methods such as hand-lines or harpoons? Why/why not?

Raising fish on farms is one alternative to wild fishing. However, fish farms also affect the environment and many farmed fish require large amounts of wild fish for food. Farmed tuna consume as much as 7.7 kilograms of wild fish for every 0.45 kilograms of growth.

ANALYSIS

What factors might alter the author's viewpoint on developing a sustainable fishing industry?

Farmed fish are usually raised packed together in an unnaturally small area. This results in the fish having more diseases, which they often pass on to wild fish swimming near the farms. Fish packed into farms also produce a lot of faeces, which pollutes the surrounding area.

VISUAL FEATURES

How would you interpret the textual information shown in the overview chart visually?

Not all fish that we can buy has been harvested in environmentally damaging ways. Tilapia is a plant-eating fish raised on farms that does not require wild fish for food. Catfish and shellfish are also farmed in ways that are less harmful to the environment. Fish caught with a hand-line or harpooned, and hand-gathered shellfish, are also much less harmful.

You can reduce the impact of your food choices on the environment by being aware of where the fish you eat has come from and choosing sustainable seafood. Local consumer fishing guides are available in most places to help you make environmentally friendly seafood choices.

FISHING METHOD	SPECIES CAUGHT	IMPACT ON MARINE HABITAT	IMPACT ON SPECIES CAUGHT
Dive Caught	Scallops, oysters	Low impact	Low impact
Hand-gathered or Raked	Clams, cockles, squids	Low impact	Low impact
Hand-line	Mackerel, cod	Low impact	Low impact
Bottom-trawling (shelf seas)	Cod, haddock, plaice, monkfish	Some impact	Medium impact
Dredge	Scallops, oysters	High impact	Medium impact
Hydraulic or Suction Dredge	Clams, cockles, squids	High impact	Medium impact
Bottom-trawling (deepwater coral reefs)	Orange roughy, skate, shark	High impact	High impact
Chemical	Grouper, snapper	High impact	High impact
Explosives	Grouper, snapper	High impact	High impact
Drift Net (high seas)	Tuna, shark	Low impact	High impact

KEY

Low impact · Some impact · Medium impact · High impact

Overview of some fishing methods available in terms of their sustainability, their impact on marine habitat and species.

Water Consumption

CLARIFY
water tables

Another way in which food production affects the environment is the use of water. Drought is a major problem facing many countries today. Twenty percent of the world's population, in 30 countries, faces water shortages. By 2025 this number is expected to rise to 30 percent of the world's population in 50 countries.

Every day 5760 people die because they don't have access to fresh water.

RESEARCH
Do you accept the author's statistics? Why/why not? What evidence can you find to support these statistics?

As water gets more and more scarce, water conservation will become an even greater environmental issue. Conserving water is not just about reducing the length of your showers or flushing the toilet less often. Considering water usage in your food choices can make a considerable difference to water conservation.

Beef production is by far the most water-consuming. One kilogram of beef requires 15,500 litres of water. Compare that with potatoes or wheat, which use 900-1300 litres per kilo.

In the United States, where the demand for beef is high, growing crops for farm animals requires nearly half of the water supply and 80 percent of the agricultural land. These animals consume 90 percent of the soy crops, 80 percent of the corn crops and 70 percent of the grain crops produced.

SERIOUS DROUGHTS AND FAMINE

VISUAL FEATURES
What effect do the design and images on this spread have on you?

WATER CONSUMPTION IN THE PRODUCTION OF FOOD

LIGHT USERS	MEDIUM USERS	BIG USERS
apple (70 litres)	1 cup of coffee (140 litres)	1 hamburger (2400 litres)
1 slice of wheat bread (40 litres)	1 egg (200 litres)	1kg cheese (5000 litres)
1kg potatoes (900 litres)	1 glass of milk (200 litres)	1 kg beef (15,500 litres)
1 cup of tea (30 litres)	1 bag potato chips (185 litres)	1kg rice (3400 litres)

After beef, cheese, lamb, pork, chicken and rice are the next greatest water users. In some dry regions, such as parts of India and China, where there isn't enough rainwater for rice crops, rice farmers pump up the groundwater. This dries out the surrounding land, making it unusable for growing other crops. Water tables in some areas have been falling as much as one metre a year or more, which could mean serious droughts and famine for these countries in the future.

MESSAGE

What in your opinion has been a major focus so far for the author and why? What message did she want to convey?

Chemical Sprays

Most fresh produce found in supermarkets is grown using chemical fertilisers and pesticide sprays, which both have harmful effects on the environment.

CLARIFY

chemical fertilisers
pesticide sprays
nitrogen
synthetic fertilisers
ammonium nitrate

Fertilisers

One of the main ingredients found in fertilisers is nitrogen, which is an essential element for plant growth. At the start of the last century, the amount of produce the land could yield was limited by the amount of nitrogen found in the soil. Different crops have different nitrogen requirements, so farmers would rotate crops, growing foods such as soybeans or other legumes that add nitrogen to the soil one season, then a crop such as corn that requires nitrogen the next.

In 1909 German scientist Fritz Haber discovered a method to take nitrogen from the atmosphere and use it to enrich soil.

Throughout the 20th century, as the demand for food grew with the population growth, nitrogen fertiliser became more and more commonly used. Farmers could cultivate their land more intensively, concentrating on just one sort of crop without needing to rotate crops.

BIAS

Do you think the author's view is biased? Why/why not?

HARMS THE ENVIRONMENT

READER RESPONSE
What is your interpretation of this information?

Fertiliser is made by combining nitrogen and hydrogen under immense heat and pressure. In order to create the heat for this reaction, massive amounts of fossil fuels are used.

In the past, nitrogen was created naturally in the soil, so modern synthetic fertilisers have increased the level of carbon emissions it takes to produce the same food.

Any fertiliser that is not absorbed by the plants also harms the environment. Some of it evaporates and eventually turns into ammonium nitrate, which is a harmful greenhouse gas. The manure and urine of farm animals raised on fertilised crops release greenhouse gases methane, nitrous oxide, ammonia and carbon dioxide into the atmosphere.

Fertilisers also leach into the water table through run-off from crop or animal farms. They enter waterways, where the high levels of nitrogen can pollute the water and cause serious health problems if it is drunk.

Pesticides

In the past, crop rotation was used to control pests and diseases that can become established in the soil over time. Plants from different families are usually prone to different pests and diseases. By regularly changing the plants grown in an area, the pest and disease cycles can be broken or limited.

In the 1940s and 1950s, large amounts of synthetic pesticides began being produced to control pests and diseases in crops that were no longer rotated. Since 1950, the use of pesticides has increased 50-fold.

POINT OF VIEW

Suggest an alternative point of view on the information presented.

Synthetic pesticides contain strong chemicals that can be harmful to people, animals and the environment. More than 98 percent of sprayed insecticides and 95 percent of herbicides affect air, water, food and animals that were not the intended target of the sprays.

Pesticides sprayed onto crop fields and used to fumigate soil can give off chemicals called **volatile organic compounds.** These chemicals can react with other chemicals to form a pollutant called ozone. About 6 percent of ozone production is from pesticides.

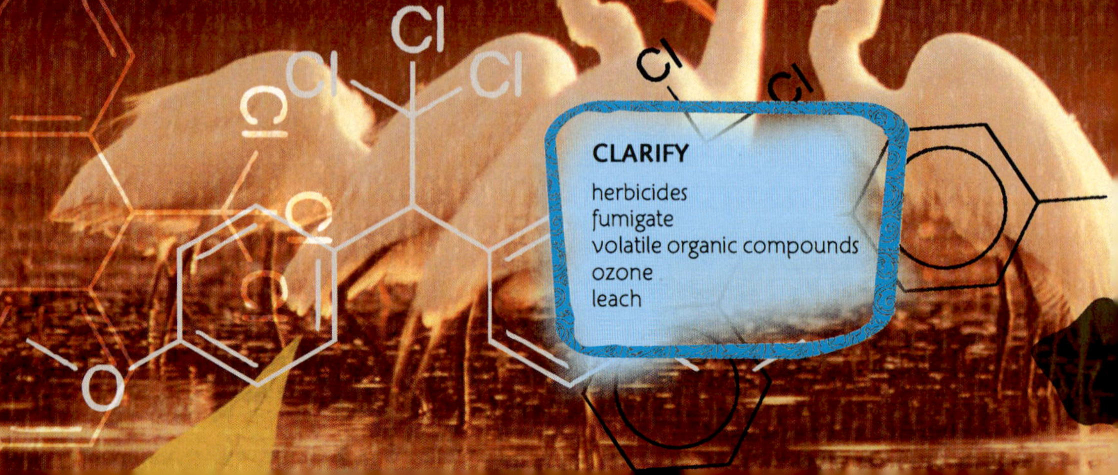

CLARIFY

herbicides
fumigate
volatile organic compounds
ozone
leach

ISSUES

Should chemical sprays be banned? Why/why not? What social action would you take to influence/inform others?

Pesticides also leach into waterways through the soil or are carried in run-off from farms. In the United States, pesticides have been found to pollute every stream and more than 90 percent of wells, affecting swimming and drinking water and killing millions of animals living in these waterways every year.

One year, on Prince Edward Island in Canada, **every fish, snake and snail** in a river near some potato farms **was killed** by pesticide run-off during heavy rains.

For the last few decades, frog populations around the world have been declining inexplicably. Many scientists believe that pesticides may be partly to blame for this decline. Pesticides used on farms have been linked to frog deaths and severe birth deformities that prevent frogs from reproducing.

Declines in bird populations have also been linked to pesticides. Pesticides affect bird populations by killing the insects and plants they eat. Birds also die from eating earthworms and insects that have been sprayed. Some pesticides can affect bird eggs when sprayed onto them, reducing the number of successful hatches. It is estimated that more than 68 million birds are killed each year in the United States by pesticides. In Europe, 116 species of birds are now threatened.

Pesticides also kill honeybees, which are essential for pollinating plants. In the United States, pesticides kill about a fifth of the honeybee colonies every year.

QUESTION GENERATE

What questions do you have about this information?

Making a Difference

Buying Organic

Buying organic food is one way of reducing the impact of food production on the environment. Organic crops are grown without the use of synthetic fertilisers and pesticides. Farmers use more traditional methods of farming, such as crop rotation and natural fertilisers and pesticides to maintain the soil and reduce pests and disease.

CLARIFY
growth hormones

Organic animals are reared without antibiotics or growth hormones and are fed a diet of pesticide- and fertiliser-free grass. Disease is controlled through more natural methods, such as rotating cattle and providing a free-range environment, which is much healthier for the animals.

Organic farm soil is of higher quality than soil that has been contaminated with fertilisers and pesticides.

QUESTION GENERATE
What questions can you generate about this information?

With more organic matter in the soil, it is better able to retain water and so produce more crops in periods of drought. Studies have shown that organic farms have yields 20 to 40 percent higher than other farms during drought periods.

FARMERS USE MORE TRADITIONAL METHODS OF FARMING, SUCH AS CROP ROTATION

RESEARCH

"Studies have shown that organic farms have yields 20 to 40 percent higher than other farms during drought periods." Do you accept the author's statistics? Why/why not? What evidence can you find to support these statistics?

Slow Food

"Slow food" is a movement that started in Italy in response to the fast food industry. It promotes a change back to traditional diets and methods of producing food.

Slow food promotes eating only locally produced, organic food and food produced with traditional and sustainable farming and fishing methods.

Regional food specialities based on local flavours and ingredients are celebrated.

The bulk of food eaten in a slow food diet is plant-based and no fast food or factory-farmed meat is eaten.

In a time when the future of the environment is under serious threat from human actions, it is essential that we consider what we eat and where it has come from.

Changing our approach to food will go a long way to reducing our impact on the environment.

QUESTION GENERATE

Has *The True Cost of Food* influenced your thinking about the effects of large-scale food production? Why/why not?

ROMOTES EATING ONLY LOCALLY PRODUCED, ORGANIC FOOD

Index

animal-based farming 3, 10-13, 18, 19, 21, 24, 26
antibiotics 12, 24
carbon footprint 8
crop
- farming 3, 13, 19, 20, 21, 22, 24, 26
- rotation 20, 22, 24

cryptosporidium 11
deforestation 2, 10, 13
drought 4, 18, 19, 24
effects of food production on
- animals 2, 4, 10, 11, 12, 14, 15, 16, 22, 23
- humans 4, 9, 10, 11, 12, 21, 22, 24

fertilisers 20-21, 24
fishing
- commercial 14-17
- fish farming 17
- sustainable seafood 17, 26

food miles 6-9
fossil fuels 6, 21
global warming 4-5, 7, 10
greenhouse gases 4, 5, 7, 10, 11, 21
land degradation 2, 13
ocean ecosystem 15, 16
organic food 24
ozone pollution 22
pesticides 20, 22-23, 24
slow food 26
super bugs 12
water
- consumption 2, 18-19, 24
- pollution 2, 10, 11, 17, 18, 21, 22, 23
- tables 19, 21

READING BETWEEN THE LINES

What inferences can you make about the author's values and beliefs? What helped you form your opinion?

THINK ABOUT THE TEXT

MAKING CONNECTIONS — what connections can you make to the information presented in **THE TRUE COST OF FOOD?**

TEXT TO SELF

- Forming opinions on food production issues
- Taking a stance on food production issues
- Exploring damage done to the environment by food production
- Thinking about what we eat and where it comes from
- Changing eating habits
- Thinking about the effects of pesticides and fertilisers
- Thinking about the waste/overfishing of marine food resources

TEXTTOTEXT/MEDIA

Discuss what connections you can make between this informational text and other media you have read or seen.

TEXTTOWORLD

Talk about situations in the world that might connect to elements in the text.

PLANNING AN INFORMATIONAL REPORT

1. RESEARCH

a. Select a TOPIC

THE TRUE COST OF FOOD PRODUCTION

b. BRAINSTORM the QUESTIONS YOU NEED TO ASK

FACTORS THAT AFFECT THE TRUE COST OF FOOD PRODUCTION

- commercial fishing?
- global warming?
- pollution from transportation?
- chemical fertilisers and sprays?
- animal farming?
- land degradation?
- deforestation?

c. Use MULTIMEDIA RESOURCES for your investigation

Internet, library, journals, television documentaries, encyclopedias, newspapers, interviews with experts/organisations, DVDs, magazines, research documents

d. SKIM-READ and TAKE NOTES

as you research.
Record the referencecs you used.
Cross-reference your data.

e. SORT through YOUR NOTES, identifying KEY INFORMATION

and what is missing or what other information you need to know. Organise your information using headings/ focus questions.

2. PLAN THE REPORT

a. Write an INTRODUCTION with an OPENING STATEMENT.

Opening statement: Behind every environmental problem, food is a contributing factor.

b. Decide on a LOGICAL ORDER for your INFORMATION

What will come first, next...last?

c. Write up your information

d. DESIGN some VISUALS to include in your report.

You can use graphs, diagrams, labels, charts, tables, cross-sections...

WRITING AN INFORMATIONAL REPORT

HAVE YOU...

* recorded important information?
* written in a formal style that is concise and accurate?
* backed up factual statements with credible evidence/details?
* used scientific or technical terms?
* written a logical sequence of facts?
* avoided unnecessary descriptive details, metaphors or similes?
* avoided author bias or opinion?
* evaluated the relevance of your factual content to the topic?

...DON'T FORGET TO REVISIT YOUR WRITING. DO YOU NEED TO CHANGE, ADD OR DELETE ANYTHING TO IMPROVE YOUR ARGUMENT?